Siona
2020

Susan Dalvi
5781

Central Reform Congregation
The Zodiac Floor

Text by Rabbi Susan Talve
Art by Siona Benjamin

Introduction

The first time I saw the symbols of the zodiac on the floor of the 6th century Bet Alpha synagogue near the Sea of Galilee, I was delighted with the playful imagery. Not only did the floor show each sign of the zodiac, but right in the center was the sun god Helios, smiling and pushing at the edges of our comfort zones with anthropomorphic images. I wanted to know if this floor and others like it were honoring the ruling culture and acknowledging that we were outsiders in our own land or a sign that we embraced aspects of other cultures as our own, without the modern fear of losing our identity to the dominant traditions surrounding us. I also love the connections in Rabbinic literature that link the astrology of the twelve zodiac signs with the 12 Hebrew months and the 12 tribes of Israel. When it was time for Central Reform Congregation to build our first building, I made sure that there would be a place for a version of the zodiac floor.

Top and bottom right: Bet Alpha is a 6th Century CE synagogue located in Israel. Bottom left: CRC floor before tile installation.

We struggled for years on a design and process for our floor. Then I met the Indian Jewish artist Siona Benjamin who embraced the vision and was willing to work on a design. As a Jewish woman born in Mumbai, Siona draws upon the Hindu, Muslim, Zoroastrian, Catholic and Buddhist influences of her home.

Examples of the art of Siona Benjamin.

4

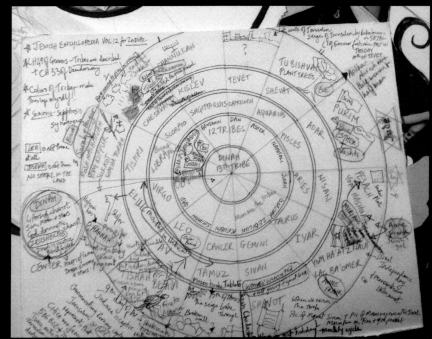

Initial Planning
Meetings

Sketches and Process

With input from our architect and original building committee, we worked for over a year on a painting that has been digitally transferred to ceramic tile. The floor was installed in the *Oneg*, a large round welcoming entry space, in August of 2015.

13

The Blue

One of the most prominent features of the floor is the artist's signature use of blue. It is the blue of the Indian god Krishna, avatar of Vishnu, a supreme god of Hinduism. It is the sacred blue of the Virgin Mary. It is also the blue of the *techelet*, the strand of blue in the ritual fringes, the *tzitzit*. It is the blue of the sea and the sky and the heavens, and the blue of the sapphire stone beneath the Holy One's throne of glory. It is the blue of the Nile in the moment before it turns to blood and the blue of the Sea of Reeds as the waters part to reveal dry land. It is a blue of expectation and a blue of redemption.

Right: Inspiration from Amar Chitra Katha comic books.
Bottom Left: Blue ritual fringes of the tallit.

Blue is also the color of the biblical Israelites who lived in Goshen apart from the Egyptians so it is the color of the other, the outsider. Today as Jews of many hues in America we are outsiders but some are also white Jews who struggle with our status and cultural identity as insiders. For our artist, Siona, the blue has become the symbol of being a Jewish woman of color who belongs everywhere and nowhere. In solidarity with the stranger, the blue makes room for all of us as we hope our Sukkat Shalom, our shelter of peace does.

15

The Sun

There are many teachings that emanate from the colorful circles of the floor. The image of the woman on the innermost circle evokes Dina, the daughter of Jacob who did not get a tribe of her own and the Shechinah – the in-dwelling of Godliness. The sun near her head connects her to the sun god found on the ancient synagogue floors created by the Jews influenced by Hellenism. The sun god may also be a symbol of the eternal and universal God of Israel, suggesting that God,(perhaps like the sun,) and not human beings, is the center of the universe. There were, however, those who worshipped the sun and believed that the sun revolved around the earth.

Direction of the Flow of the Floor

Hebrew speakers may be confused by the direction of the holidays, months and signs around the floor. Because Hebrew is written from right to left, the months written in Hebrew and the flow of the holidays may appear to go in the opposite direction of what one may expect. We thought about the value of living "counter clockwise" and "counter culture" that we often lift up at CRC but decided on the western ordering of clockwise to make it easier for those visiting to find their way around the circle. The Bet Alpha floor is counterclockwise.

The Holiday Cycle

The floor is filled with hidden faces, moons and other symbols that spark discussion and deepen our understanding of how the holidays are connected and how they can be meaningful in our lives today.

The Jewish holidays represent a circle dance through the seasons and our story as a people. We can begin at *Rosh Hashanah*, the new moon of the 7th month of *Tishrei*. This is our New Year but our Torah reading is not the beginning of Genesis and the story of creation. Instead we struggle with Genesis chapters 21 and 22, two of the most challenging stories of internal family conflict.

On our floor we represent the holiday of *Rosh Hashanah* with the mothers in these chapters, *Hagar* and *Sarah* sharing a third eye. Their sons, *Ishmael* and *Isaac*, are put at risk by their common father *Abraham* and by the rivalry of their mothers. The third eye is also known as the inner eye and is a mystical concept that refers to an ability to see beyond ordinary sight. The third eye chakras provide the energy for spiritual reflection and insight and encourage clear thought.

In Siona's bold painting, *Sarah* and *Hagar* represent the Jewish and Muslim mothers who have lost their sons to generations of conflict. They share respective head coverings and challenge us with the prominent red drop that is either the blood of the conflict or a symbol of our common bloodline. On our floor, they are, we are, sisters.

The red drop remains a theme throughout the floor and reminds us that the bloodline runs deep through the 12 tribes of the central circle and the reclaimed tribe of the daughter of *Jacob, Dina*, who fills the center of the floor with her invitation to join the circle dance.

Rosh Hashanah leads us through the *Days of Awe* to the growing moon of *Yom Kippur*, a day that requires us to take responsibility for our sins and the sins of the world represented by the scapegoat. The scapegoat reminds us that we can blame others for the brokenness we experience in the world or we can stand together and collectively recommit to our purpose of *Tikkun Olam*, the repair of the world.

The fragile *sukkah* reminds us that there are no walls high or strong enough to keep us safe if the whole world does not become a *sukkat shalom*, a shelter of peace. The full moon of *sukkot* shines a light through the thatched roof of the *sukkah*. The thatching of the roof both conceals and reveals. The *sukkah* on our floor is a suggestion of a shelter and seems transparent; it holds the images of these holy days within itself.

The end of the holy day cycle brings us to *Simchat Torah*, with the Sephardic style *tik* holding the Torah scroll calling us to "*Shema*," to listen to the end of Deuteronomy and, in the next moment, to hear the beginning of Genesis. We begin the cycle of reading the Torah again. We change the prayers for dew begun at *Pesach* to the prayers for rain and the drops become the healing and purifying waters of the rain from the full spiraled clouds present in the *Shemini Atzeret* sky.

The next holiday as we travel the floor is *Hanukkah*. The *Hanukkiah* (eight branched menorah) is brought together with the story of *Judith* and *Holofernes*. This story opens conversations on the use of military force and the question of sacrificing some lives to save others. The story is found in the *Book of Judith* in the *Apocrypha* and is ascribed to the second or early first centuries BCE.

The beautiful widow *Judith* uses her charm to overcome the Assyrian general. She comes from the town of *Bethulia*, related to the Hebrew word for virgin, that stands strategically on the route to Jerusalem. When the men of the town are ready to give up, *Judith* convinces them to trust their faith in God who will help her defeat the enemy. She prays to God to help her bring the enemy down with the deceit of her lips and the hand of a woman. The lights of *Hanukkah* brighten the *Kislev* sky but do not reduce the story to a tale of simple miracles.

The holiest day in the Jewish calendar is *Shabbat*. Each week from sundown on Friday to sundown on Saturday we are given a taste of the world to come with this gift of time. The lighting of the candles is the sign that *Shabbat* begins.

When I told Siona that we chose the symbol of the blessing hands for the logo of CRC and that I wanted them to be in the floor she immediately began to envision the *mudras*. A *mudra* is a spiritual gesture that encourages the flow of spiritual energy. When performed with the hands they represent healing and wholeness. There are normally twelve mudras. This complements the twelve months, the twelve zodiac signs, the twelve main holidays and the twelve tribes that are also found in the floor design.

Eve becomes the tree of *TuBishvat*, the new year of the trees. With her roots and her wings she evokes the popular teaching that we must give both to our children. The pomegranate celebrates the wisdom acquired by her act of eating the fruit by connecting it to the tradition that its seeds represent the 613 commandments that we perform to draw godliness into the world. This suggests that *Eve* liberated us from the Garden of Eden through another tree, the Tree of Knowledge, that our lives would have purpose in repairing the broken world outside of the garden. We are the caretakers of creation and of the survival of our planet. *Eve* has the top of the pomegranate in one of her many mudra-hands with a side view of the six pointed star that has become a symbol for the Jewish people.

In our cycle it becomes clear that *Purim* is our last fling of abandon. The tradition is to put on masks and get so drunk we cannot tell the difference between *Haman* and *Mordechai*, the villain and the hero. The *Megillat Esther*, the scroll of *Esther*, tells the unlikely tale of a beauty queen who saves her people by first hiding and then revealing her identity as a Jew. The illustrated Scroll of *Esther*, also created by the artist Siona Benjamin, adorns the Southern wall of the synagogue.

On *Purim* we learn what is God and not God. *Vashti*, the wife of the king who is rejected because she refused to dance naked in front of her husband's drunken court, remains in the story to make sure that what happened to her will not happen to *Esther*. She is the protector of *Esther* and adds a feminist midrashic twist to the story. The mask of *Esther* gives us the opening to explore our own masks and the reasons we wear them. Throughout our history we have hidden behind many masks including changing our names and our noses to fit in.

The Scroll of *Esther* is adorned by *Haman* and *Mordecai,* who represent the different sides of our nature as human beings. Within us are the *yetzer ha-ra* and the *yetzer ha-tov*, the not so good and the good inclinations that challenge us to choose the blessing and to choose life. There is no mention of God in the Book of *Esther* suggesting that God is everywhere and in everything, even in suffering.

The beard of the evil *Haman* becomes the redemptive flowing hair of *Miriam*. One of the five full moons is in her hair and her tambourine holds the *Seder* plate with its symbols both ancient and modern.

The orange on the *Seder* plate reminds us that the story of the Exodus is not a history lesson frozen in time but an on-going narrative meant to inspire each of us to feel that we were there at the sea and that we are continually adding our voices and wisdom to the ongoing story of the Torah.

The Red Sea separates or connects *Purim* to *Passover*. There can be no *Passover* without the last fling of *Purim*, our Mardi Gras, that takes us from our adolescence to becoming a people with a purpose. The horse drowning in the sea reminds us that the price of our freedom was great and that the angels could not sing our freedom song because there was still suffering. We are forced to ask if the price of one people's freedom must be on the backs of others, this time the Egyptian people. Is the sea that is blood red giving birth or taking lives? Is it a birth canal for the *erev rav*, the mixed multitudes becoming a people with a unique identity, or a reminder that until all can be free, none can be free.

Passover and the *Omer* are another example of how Siona resisted the kind of predictable linear art that we are used to seeing. The plagues bleed into the *Omer* period and one has to take in the *yartzeit* candle, the pink triangle, the symbols of *Yom ha-Shoah* and *Yom ha-Atzma-ut* with the fires of *Lag B'Omer* –all together. The fires are between the plagues recalling the tradition that the great plague in the time of *Rabbi Akiva* ended on *Lag B'Omer*. The forty-nine days of the *Omer* flow into the climax of the story with *Ruth* opening her mouth to the future of hope with her powerful words of commitment to *Naomi*. The sheaves of wheat teach us that the corners of our fields belong to the poor and the entire image is held in the arms of the Torah.

23

Before we arrive at the summer months that bring holy days of destruction and mourning we have inserted the reminder that each month there is a celebration of *Rosh Hodesh*, the new moon. The woman of gold is watching the melting of the golden calf as a commentary on how the women who would not give up their gold did so to keep us from committing the greatest sin– idolatry; the sin of certainty symbolized by the solid calf built out of fear rather than out of faith and hope. The window shows the new moon and the light bulb as an acknowledgment that modern Jewish women have reclaimed the celebration of *Rosh Hodesh* to hold conversations of our connections to the moon and her cycles.

The summer months bring the *17th of Tammuz*, the three weeks and the *9th of Av*. Before the cycle can begin again we must mourn the losses and missed opportunities of the past year. In these frames we see the destruction of Jerusalem and the presence of the Golden Dome and the Al Aqsa mosque that today must remain unthreatened if there is to be peace– perhaps even for the promise that the messiah will be born, one of the traditions of *Tisha b'Av*. The messianic figure on our floor is non-binary and gender inclusive. The full moon of *Tu B'av*, the Jewish Valentine's Day, is also depicted with a hidden heart.

Finally, the month of *Elul* comes with the shofar, more mudras, the plural word *Chaim* (life), and *Hannah*, the great mother, birthing the new year, ready to call us into the cycle of hope and the possibility of transformation and something new, again.

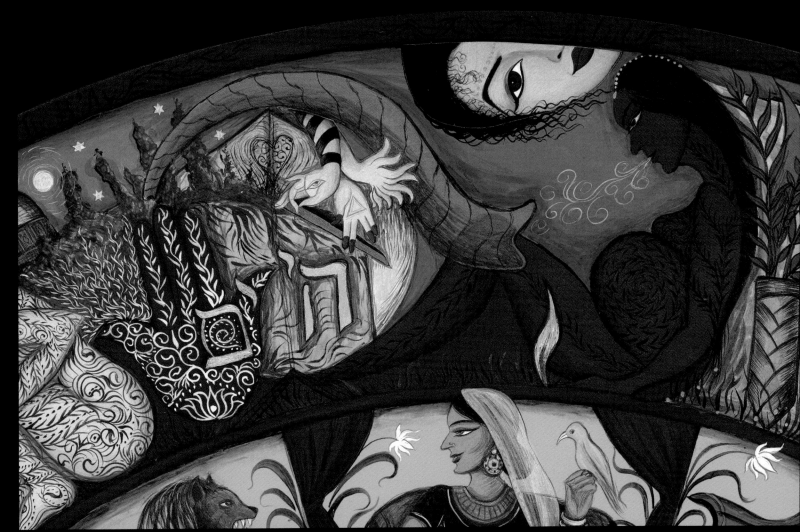

The Zodiac

Astrology is the influence of the stars on human events and the predictions based on this study. The zodiac depicts a zone in the heavens that contains the paths of the sun, the moon and the planets. The 12 signs were developed by the Chaldean astronomers.

The Bible and Apocrypha mention the diviner and soothsayer (Lev. 19:26 and Deut. 18:10). The prophets were aware of the practices of the star gazers. In the book of Daniel they are negatively referred to as *Chaldeans* and *Kasdim*. But Josephus writes that astrology was common among the Jews in his day and that the Jewish misinterpretation of the signs was responsible for the revolt against the Romans (Jewish Wars 6:288).

In the Talmud, the majority of the sages believed in the role played by the celestial bodies in determining human affairs. However, there is also an attempt to rise above predetermined destiny. King Solomon was said to have known astrology (Ecclesiastes Rabbah 7:23).

In several places it says that every person has a *mazal*, a particular star, which is their patron from conception and birth (Shabbat 53:b and BK 2b). We say *"mazal tov"* for congratulations, in celebration of our stars being aligned and working as they should!

The artist's Zodiac designs were influenced by the Jantar Mantar astronomical monuments in Jaipur, India, which the artist and author visited together.

Two people born under the same star have a bodily and spiritual kinship (Nedarim 39b and BM 30b). Not only are human beings influenced by the stars but there is not a blade of grass that does not have its star in the heavens to tell it to grow! The Talmud also teaches about the power and meaning of eclipses (Sukkot 29).

One of my favorite Talmudic passages gives a formula to change one's destiny if you feel that your stars are just not right! (B. meg.3a).

In the Middle Ages there were Jewish books written on astrology. Ibn Ezra had astrological manuscripts though we are not sure if he wrote them or translated them. There was a Persian Jewish astrologer, Andruzgar b. Zadi Farouk in the 9th century, and Abu Daud from Bagdad at the beginning of the 10th century who all studied the stars.

Saadia Gaon in his commentary on the Sefer Yetzirah has astrological material and Ibn Ezra suggested that the *urim* and *thummim* of the high priests were astrological instruments.

The 12th century philosopher, Maimonides, rejected astrology as superstition. He called it "no science at all," but this did not deter other commentators, even in the future. The Kabbalistic literature has many references to astrology. The seven Hebrew letters that take a dagesh are related to the seven planets, and the seven days of the week. The twelve simple consonants are related to the twelve astrological signs and the twelve months. The Zohar and the Sefer Yetzirah, both books of Jewish mysticism, seem to take astrology for granted. Jews put our own spin on the zodiac teachings. Astrological symbols were used by the Hellenized Jews to describe the cosmic order. God is at the center and it is God's will that orders the cosmos and the stars. It is God that responds to prayer and controls and shapes the influence of astrology in our lives.

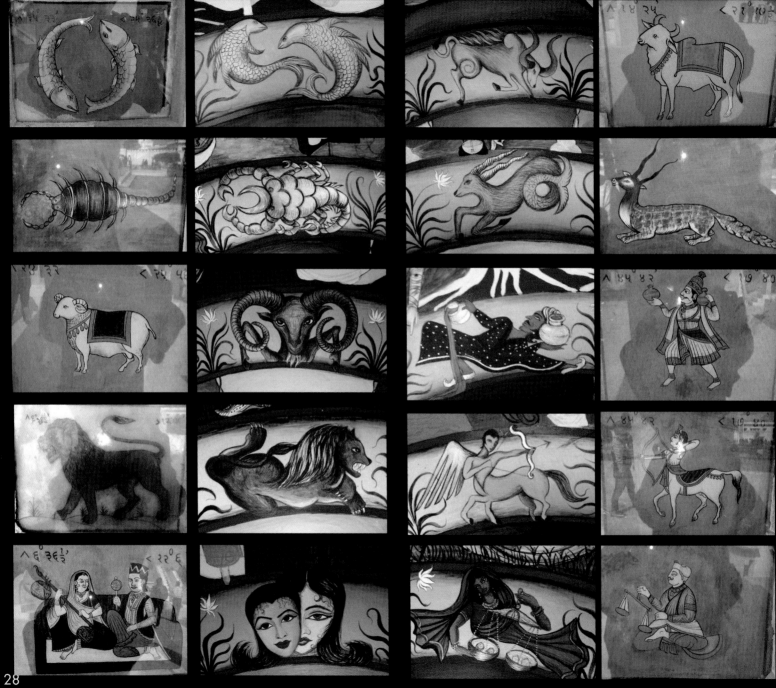

28

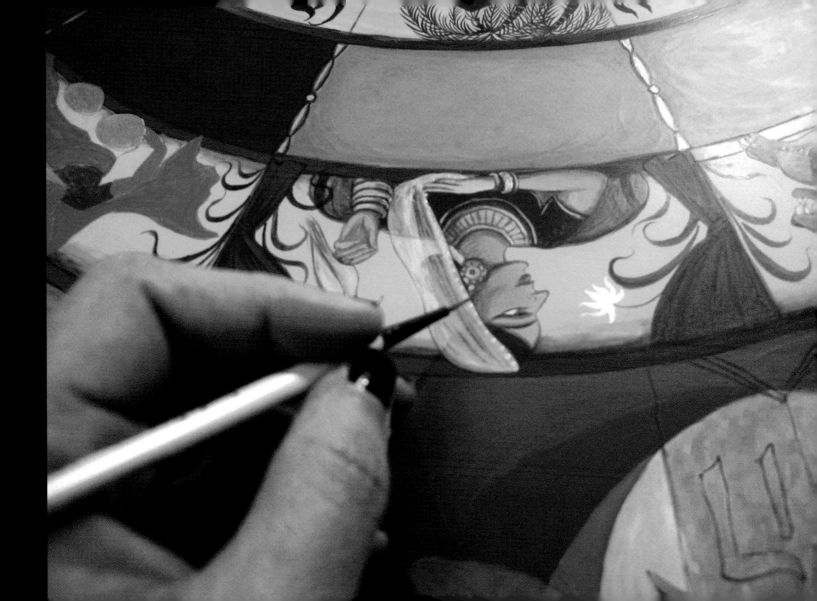

30

The St. Louis Art Community is invited to

Breakfast with the Artist

Join Central Reform Congregation and Rabbi Susan Talve
as we welcome artist and scholar

Siona Benjamin

Thursday, June 9 at CRC
8:00 · 9:30 in the morning
5020 Waterman Boulevard, 63108

Be inspired by the artistic process,
rich symbolism, and
profound intersectionality.

To RSVP please contact Tristan at
tristan@centralreform.org or 314·361·1564 ext. 100.

We hope that the beauty of the Zodiac floor inspires all who experience the color, content and creativity of its many circles and layers of learning. May it inspire us to open to the inclusivity and spirit of possibility that will help make the world a more loving, holy and colorful place for all.

Rabbi Susan Talve and artist Siona Benjamin at the
Central Reform Congregation in St. Louis
www.centralreform.org   www.artsiona.com

ISBN: 978-0-578-75963-0 (print)
ISBN: 978-0-578-75964-7 (e-book)

Printed by IngramSpark in the United States of America.

Published by
Central Reform Congregation
5020 Waterman Blvd.
St. Louis, MO 63108

www.centralreform.org